IMAGES OF ENGLAND

LEE-ON-THE-SOLENT

A postcard from the fifties. The definite article is missing from the name, as it frequently was in advertisements and commerical publications. In 1894 the Newton Robinson family named the new resort Lee-on-the-Solent and so it is today.

IMAGES OF ENGLAND

LEE-ON-THE-SOLENT

NORMAN ELLIS

First published in 1997 by Tempus Publishing

Reprinted in 2008 by The History Press
The Mill, Brimscombe Port,
Stroud, Gloucestershire, GL5 2QG
www.thehistorypress.co.uk

Reprinted 2013

Copyright © Lesley A. Burton and Beryl F. Peacey, 1997, 2008

ISBN 978 0 7524 1038 8

Typesetting and origination by
The History Press.
Printed and bound in England.

This postcard from the twenties gives a nice flavour of the resort as the place to be for aspiring bathing belles.

Contents

Foreword

I have lived in Lee-on-the-Solent all my life, apart from an enforced period during the Second World War, and I would not want to live anywhere else. Back in the thirties my grandfather Mr Alfred Prestidge built the Lee Tower complex and, in doing so, made Lee-on-the-Solent different from most of the seaside resorts along the South coast. It was very sad for my family when it was deemed necessary to pull it down and deprive Lee of its uniqueness.

An aunt, who lived in London, visited my grandparents, using the passenger train which ran from Gosport to Lee until 1931, getting off at Browndown Halt. I remember my mother lifting me up so that I could watch the last train leave, we lived on Portsmouth Road then. A section of Lee library was used as a school room during the war and before my evacuation to the country, I attended classes there.

Many others will have recollections of 'Old Lee' and I am sure they will feel as nostalgic as I do.

Joan Hadley

Map showing development of Lee and the considerable encroachment of the airfield complex.

Introduction

A picture is worth a thousand words, so goes the old adage and, as such, form the basis on which books like this must earn their popularity. Lee-on-the-Solent is a relatively young community if viewed in terms of most historic towns. It emerged as a seaside-cum-watering place little more than a century ago and then almost by accident.

In 1884 a Mr C.E. Robinson was cruising in the Solent and through his binoculars liked what he saw of the coastline. It seemed to him that the green clifflands and gently shelving beach might have all the potential for a resort development. He persuaded his wealthy, businessman father, Sir John Newton Robinson of Newton Manor, Swanage, Dorset, to buy up this attractive coastal strip. Father and son planned to develop Lee as a health and seaside resort to rival Southsea and Bournemouth. Their limited company invested huge sums of money in promoting and developing the new resort of Lee-on-the-Solent. Prior to 1884, and the advent of the Newton Robinson family, Lee was a tiny hamlet with a thinly scattered population engaged in farming and fishing. Its name derived from an Old English word for a clearing in the forest.

The name Manor Way gives a clue as to Lee's ancient history. A great manor house and associated farms stood here in medieval times. Gilbert Le Breton was their probable owner. The family had connections with Binstead in the Isle of Wight. Quarr Abbey, Rowner church and Winchester cathedral were all built with the stone quarried at Binstead, as was the great manor house at Lee. It was badly damaged by fire and Le Breton farm house is thought to be the smaller replacement house for the family.

The Lee-on-the-Solent of today stands as a testament to a Victorian pipe-dream. Plots were rapidly bought up and developed by speculative builders. Many substantial Victorian villas off Manor Way are an enduring reminder of our forefathers' love of decoration and fine craftsmanship.

The early sale catalogues for the new resort make fascinating reading. Queen and empire are invoked in order to persuade the affluent middle class paterfamilias to part with his money. Having done so, he and his family could enjoy unrivalled views of the Solent and the Isle of Wight where the Queen herself had a much loved house at Osborne.

The Newton Robinson's visionary scheme was, at first, a gratifying success. The phrase 'Victorian values' is frequently displayed by politicians of all shades of opinion to explain a particular ethos which is often thought to be lacking in today's society. One marked aspect of our forebearers was their energy and enterprise in embracing new ideas which they managed to combine with a degree of altruism. The concept of Lee-on-the-Solent as a health resort with substantial family houses and a fine pier for exercise and recreation is a good example of those Victorian values.

The future must have seemed rosy. The Queen was about to celebrate her diamond jubilee, the mighty British Empire prevailed and the monied classes responded to the Newton Robinson challenge.

The building of houses, shops, hotels and other commercial premises proceeded at a brisk rate. Meanwhile, plans for a pier were put into operation. No self-respecting Victorian resort was complete without one of these. Lady Newton Robinson had laid the foundation stone in

1885 and three years later the 750 foot long pier was finished at a cost of £10,000. It provided an attractive amenity for locals and holiday makers alike, as well as enabling steamers to carry both passengers and freight across to the Isle of Wight.

In May 1894, the newly formed Lee-on-the-Solent Light Railway Company opened the line from Fort Brockhurst to the pier. Light Railway regulations stipulated a maximum speed of 25 miles per hour only. This leisurely pace undoubtedly added to the enjoyment of passengers as the train wound slowly along the curving coastline so close to the sea with the lovely Solent and Isle of Wight views. Short though the journey may have been, just twelve minutes between Brockhurst and Lee pier, it had three classes of travel, from 9d. to 3d.

It is a sad but indisputable fact that the first fine careless rapture of the Lee-on-the-Solent enterprise began to wane soon after the First World War. Large scale investment of any significance ground almost to a halt in the twenties, war office and Admirality's use of land to the east of Browndown and to the west at what would become the Naval Air Station Daedalus precluded further expansion. Between the wars, however, older people remember Lee with affection. The settlement of families encouraged the establishment of tea rooms, small cafes, while an attractive High Street with a variety of interesting specialist shops catering for the community's every requirement. In this period, too, the pier pavilion was the focus for much of the light entertainment for both residents and holiday makers. Some older readers may well remember the tea dances held in the Pier Ballroom. The actor and playwright, Noel Coward, made his theatrical debut on the pier bandstand rather earlier in 1911 at the age of 12 while on a holiday visit with his family at Hillhead.

By the late twenties, the residents of Lee were feeling isolated from their larger neighbours at Gosport, itself achieving borough status in 1922. In 1928, Lee rate payers petitioned Gosport Borough Council for amalgamation. The wording of the petition is worth repeating:
'Lee will be in close touch with the local governing body and can thus give more articulate expression to its hopes and ideals. The wider powers of a municipal body will provide that "fillip" to development which Lee needs at this juncture'.

In view of the post-1945 decline of Lee, the irony of the amalgamation will not be lost on today's residents.

For a time in the thirties, the future looked more promising. In December 1935, the Lee Tower complex was officially opened. Built to a handsome, Art-Deco style, typical of the period, the Tower appeared to symbolise the hopes and aspirations of the petitioning ratepayers. Three years earlier, the pier pavilion had been badly damaged by fire and there were hopes that the impetus provided by the Tower's success would lead to the pier's rehabilitation.

At the beginning of the Second World War, however, the army destroyed the pier as a precaution against invasion. The Tower never lived up to its developers' expectations for the revitalising of Lee and as a building complex it was both reviled and admired in equal proportions. It lost money on a heroic scale and was finally demolished in 1969, leaving the sea front flat and featureless. With the benefit of hindsight and today's much more enlightened attitude towards styles of architecture the Tower would almost certainly be awarded a 'listed' commendation by the Department of National Heritage.

The end of the rainbow, perhaps for Lee? Walking around the town today, it is still possible to experience a ghostly reminder of the Victorian splendour imagined by the enterprising Newton Robinson family. The town too, has some thirties' buildings of real merit. Old photographs and ephemera from the past enable the reader to re-capture something of Lee-on-the-Solent in its brief hey-day. New photographs had been included where they have a relevance to the changed face of the development of Lee today. Lee-on-the-Solent is, after all, only just over a century old.

We can only hope that the contents of this book will touch a chord and recall that even at the end of a rainbow, the sunshine stays!

Lesley Burton and Beryl Peacey, July 1997

One

The New Resort

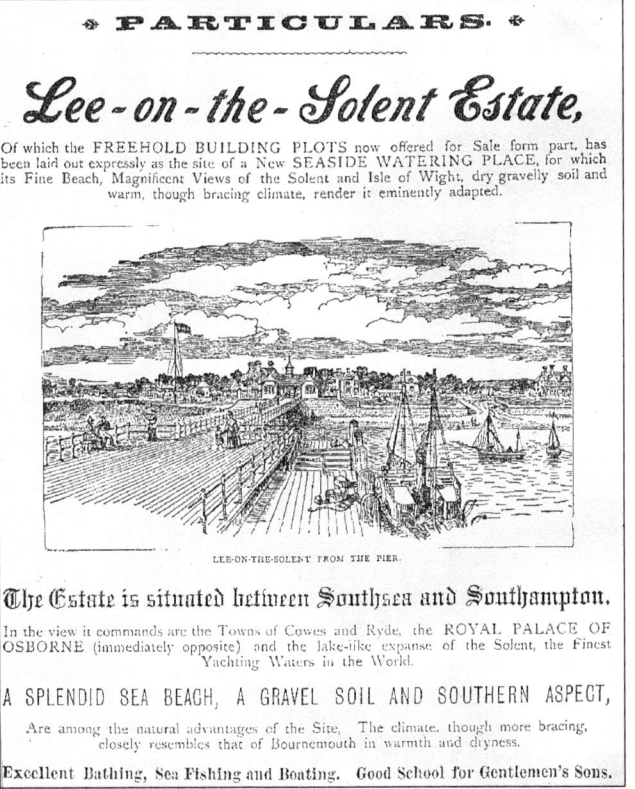

A copy of the original catalogue of freehold building plots for sale in the new watering place to be known as Lee-on-the-Solent.

The early years of this century on the Cliffs. Note the canvas-style tents or beach huts and the Victorian-style push chair awaiting its small occupant.

One of the earliest photographs of Lee. The pier was designed as an integral part of Lee as a watering place. Here we see work in progress. The pier was finished in 1888 and measured 750 feet long.

The pier head, c. 1905.

Looking towards the pier head, showing the Pier Hotel and people lounging in deck chairs in the twenties. It cannot be very hot, for the people strolling towards the camera are warmly dressed!

The pier, looking west, with the railway station and line to the right and what appears to be a car on the beach, c. 1920.

Catastrophe struck the pier in 1932. Faulty electrical wiring destroyed the popular pavilion at the end of the pier. It was never replaced and the Admiralty removed the remainder of the pier at the outbreak of the Second World War.

Looking west from the top of Lee Tower. This thirties' photograph shows the popularity of the beach and Clifflands with the putting green in the right foreground.

A view looking east from the Lee Tower, in the thirties. Skippers' garage is to the left of the picture. Note the cars parked right down on the water's edge.

13

A ground level view looking east along the Clifflands. Lee Tower has gone and Skippers' garage has been replaced by a seventies' block of flats.

Looking west along the front. This is possibly a pre-war photograph as road and promenade are clear of traffic.

Lee beach and promenade, close to the Elmore Sailing Club, in the sixties.

Marine Parade West, with Milvil Road on the right. A traffic-free photograph from the late twenties, with the entrance to the putting green and gardens on the left.

The groynes and sea wall of the old familiar sea front. Two boys who will not be able to try these spectacular leaps from the new promenade.

The new beach, contractors still at work levelling the stones.

Two

The Romance of Rail

The single line from Fort Brockhurst to Lee was officially opened in May 1894. There were halts at Fort Gomer, Browndown and Elmore. Maximum speed for the fifteen minute journey was 25 miles per hour and there were three prices; 3d, 6d and 9d. The line was never commercially viable, closing to passengers in 1931 and goods in 1935.

Lee-on-the-Solent Railway

TRAIN SERVICE BETWEEN
Lee-on-the-Solent & Fort Brockhurst Junction (L.& S.W.R.)

1st JUNE to 30th SEPTEMBER, 1908 (or until further notice).

FROM LEE-ON-THE-SOLENT

STATIONS		WEEK DAYS.								SUNDAYS.				
		a.m.	a.m.	a.m.	p.m.	p.m.	p.m	p.m.	p.m.	p.m.	p.m	p.m.	p.m.	p.m.
Lee-on-the-Solent ...	dep.	9.20	10.35	11.50	2.10	2.50	4.10	6.30	7.30	3.0	4.35	...	6.40	
Browndown	..	...	Stop	by	sig	nal			...	Stop	by	sig	nal	
Privett ...	..	..		do.	do.					...	do.	do.		
Fort Brockhurst Junction	arr.	9.35	10.50	12. 5	2.25	3. 5	4.25	6.45	7.45	3.15	4.50	...	6.55	
Fort Brockhurst Junction	dep.	9.45	10.54	12.11	2.39	3.29	4.46	7.19	8.49	3.24	5.4		7. 9	
Fareham ...	arr.	9.51	11 0	12.17	2.45	3.35	4.52	7.25	8.57	3.30	5.10		7 15	
Eastleigh ...	,.	10.24	11.24	12.43	3.14	...	5.18	7.58	9.33	...	5.43		8 0	
Salisbury ...	.,	11.29	...	2.8	4.23	4.57	6.34	9.39	...	5.17			9.19	
Southampton ..	,.	10.46	11.49	1.09	3c29	4c10	5 42	8.28	10.19	...	6.17		8.25	
Winchester ...	,.	10.54	11.53	1. 6	3.43	...	5.47	8.31	10. 9	...	6.19		8.34	
Basingstoke ...	,,	11.26	12.25	1.36	4.19	...	6.25	9. 1	10 39	...	6.56		9.6	
London (Waterloo)	,,	12.28	1. 31	2.45	5.40	7A1	7.31	10. 5	11.48		8.40		9A59	
Fort Brockhurst Junction .	dep.	10.12	11.27	12.24	3.10	4.19	4.44	6.50	8. 5	4.2	5.37	...	7.47	
Gosport	arr.	10.15		12.27	3.13	4.22	...	6.53	8. 8	4.5	5.40	...	7.50	
Gosport Road (Alverstoke)	,,	10.28	11.31	...	...	4.48	...							
Stokes Bay ...	,,	10.32	11.35	...	...	4.53	...							
Ryde Pier Head..	,,	11. 5	12. 0	...	...	5.25	...							

TO LEE-ON-THE-SOLENT.

STATIONS		WEEK DAYS									SUNDAYS.		
		a.m.		a.m.	a.m.	a.m.	p.m.	p.m.	p.m.	p.m.	a.m.		p.m.
London (Waterloo) ...	dep.	7a10	...	7.40	9.20	11.40	...	2.20	4a12	5a30	...	10.0	...
Basingstoke ...	,,	7.50	...	9.32	10.41	12.46	...	3.33	4.37	6.12	...	11.42	...
Winchester ...	,,	8.34	...	10.3	11.11	1.15	...	4. 2	5.8	6.45	...	12.15	... 5.30
Southampton ...	,,	8.50	...	10.28	11.50	12.55	2.15	3.50	5.50	6.20	...	3c0	5 38
Salisbury ...	,,	7.47	...	8 50	10.59	12.42	1.12	3.20	4.22	6.33	...	2.15	4.59
Eastleigh ...	,,	9.12	...	10.45	12.15	1.30	...	4.16	5.40	7.21	...	12.50	6.5
Fareham ...	,,	10.5	...	11.20	12.38	2.3	3.3	4.37	6.43	7.58	...	3.55	6.33
Fort Brockhurst Junction...	arr.	10.11	...	11.26	12.44	2.9	3.9	4.43	6.49	8.4	...	4.1	... 6.39
Ryde Pier Head ...	dep.	9.8	...	10.10	11.15	...	2.0	4.0	...	6.15			
Stokes Bay ...	,,	9.35	...	10.45	11.53	...	2.30	4.37	5.15	7. 0			
Gosport Road (Alverstoke)	,,	9.39	..	10.49	11.57	...	2.34	4.41	5.19	7. 4	...		..
Gosport	,,	10.5	...		12.7	2.5	3.25	..	5.50	7.15		3.20	... 6.10
Fort Brockhurst Junction...	arr.	10.8	...	10.53	12.10	2.8	3.28	4.45	5.53	7.18	...	3.23	6.13

STATIONS		a.m.	a.m.	a.m.	a.m.	p.m.	p.m.	p.m.	p.m.	p.m.	p.m.	p.m.	p.m.	p m.
Fort Brockhurst Junction	dep.	10.15	...	11.30	12.55	2.30	3 50	4.55	7. 5	8. 5		4. 5	4.55	7. 0
Privett ...		...		Stop		by		sig	nal		Stop	by	sig	nal
Browndown ...		...		...	do.	do.		..	...	...		do.	do.	...
Lee-on-the-Solent	arr.	10.30	...	11.45	1 10	2.45	4. 5	5.10	7.20	8 20		4.20	5.10	7.15

C Southampton West.   A London Passengers by these Trains, travel via Meon Valley Line.

NOTICE.—The published Time Tables of the Lee-on-the-Solent Railway Company are only intended to fix the time before which the trains will not start, and the Company do not undertake that the trains shall start or arrive at the time specified in the Tables, nor do they guarantee the connection of trains at the various Junctions. The Company give notice that they will not be responsible for any loss, inconvenience, or expense which may arise from delay or detention, or from non-correspondence of trains at the Junctions. The times of arrival and departure of the L. & S.W. Trains at Fort Brockhurst & other Stations are given for information only & the Lee-on-the-Solent Company do not hold themselves responsible for the accuracy of same.

FARES :—

From Fort Brockhurst to Lee-on-the-Solent & vice versa—1st Class 9d., 2nd Class 6d., 3rd Class 3d.

Through Day Return Tickets are issued from Lee-on-the-Solent to Portsmouth and vice versa, (via Floating Bridge Co. and Tramway to Station Road, Brockhurst; Passengers should allow 20 minutes from Gosport Hard)—Fares 1st Class 1/11; 2nd Class 1/5; Third Class 10d.

Passengers can also book through to and from Principal L. & S. W. Stations.

E. A. ROBINSON, Manager.

H. W. Duffett, Printer, High Street, Fareham.

The coming of the railway opened up the new resort to visitors from the metropolis just as Newton Robinson had envisaged.

An attractive view of the beach showing the close proximity between sea and rail, *c.* 1905.

The Leas, looking west, with the railway line on the right and Skippers' garage with accommodation for fifty cars.

Marine Parade looking remarkably deserted except for the train, cyclist and pedestrian, c. 1910.

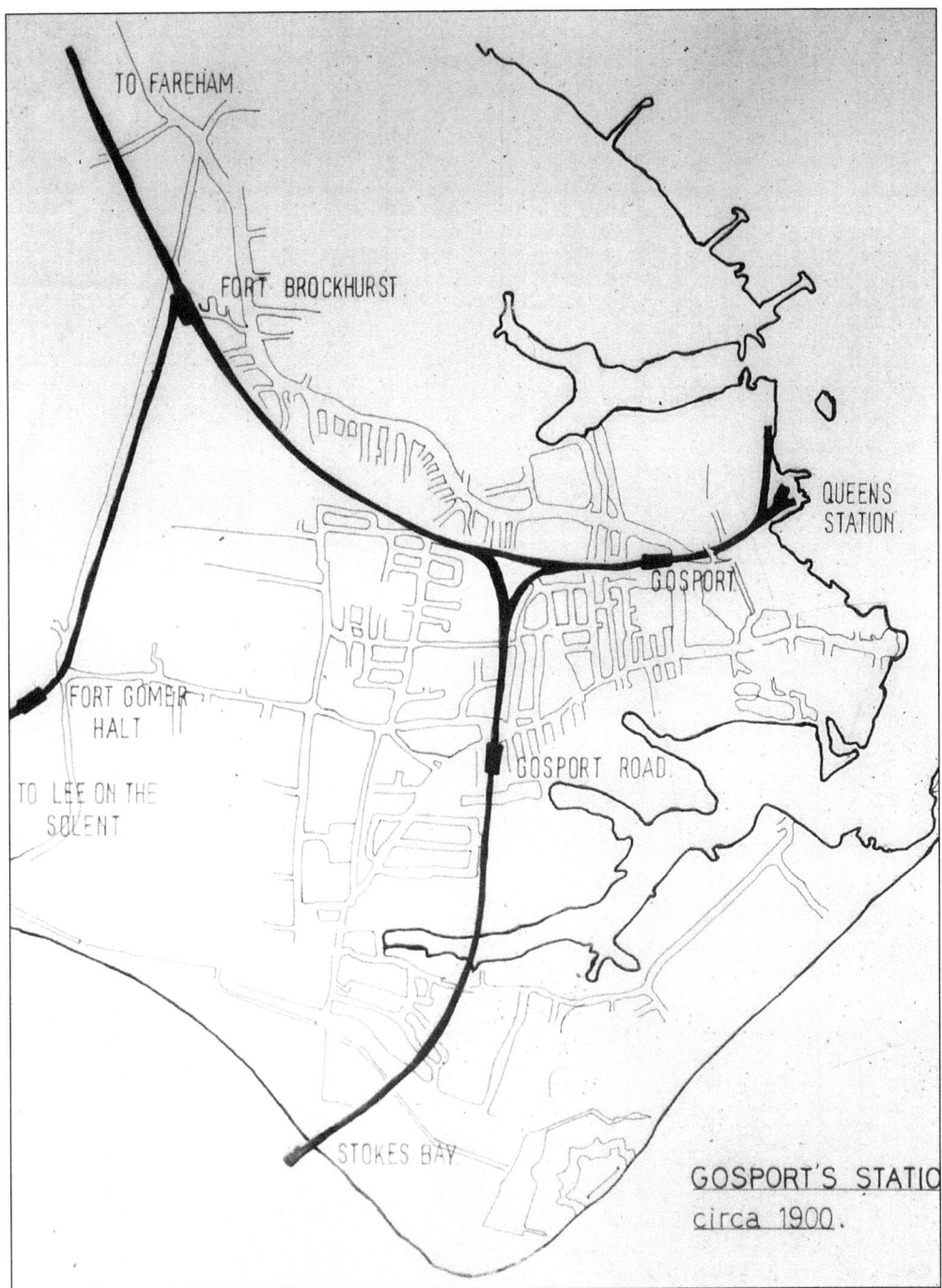

The main station at Spring Garden Lane, Gosport, opened in 1841. The Queen's station, shown on the right of the diagram, was inside Royal Clarence Yard. From there, the Queen and her family sailed to Osborne, Isle of Wight. Branch lines soon followed. The Lee branch line was particularly attractive, because it followed the coastline once past Fort Gomer Halt and gave its passengers splendid views of the Isle of Wight as they journeyed towards their holiday destination.

❧ RAILWAY COMMUNICATION ❧

WITH

LEE-ON-THE-SOLENT.

· ·

By reference to the Map of the District it will be seen that there are at present no less than Four Railway Stations within easy reach of LEE-ON-THE-SOLENT by Road, namely—

Stokes Bay (3 miles), Fareham (4½ miles), Brockhurst (2½ miles), and Gosport Road.

Fast Trains run to Fareham Station from Waterloo in two hours and twenty minutes.

Communication is kept up twice daily (except Sundays) throughout the year with Fareham Station by Omnibus.

The Fareham and Netley Railway, constructed by the L. & S.W. Railway Company, has brought Lee-on-the-Solent into direct communication with Southampton, *via* Fareham.

But the existing Railway facilities will be greatly improved by the making of the New

Lee-on-the-Solent Railway

From BROCKHURST STATION of the L. & S.W. Railway Co. to LEE-ON-THE-SOLENT, where there is a Terminal Station close to the Pier.

Brockhurst is connected with Gosport by an existing Tramway.

The Lee-on-the-Solent Light Railway campaign's publicity material for the exciting new project.

Three

Sports and Leisure

A cheerful postcard dating from the twenties. The bathing belle has her camera at the ready, plus a fashion magazine for holiday reading.

An open-topped 'bus on its way to Lee with a selection of well-dressed passengers, *c.* 1918.

A closed-top 'bus waits outside the Pier Hotel. The conductor and driver appear to be the same as in the picture above. Many local people remember the congenial operator 'Bussy Smith' who ran a single decker blue 'bus between the wars.

Lee beach and Clifflands in the early thirties. It is clear from this photograph that all the age groups are enjoying the beach and green cliff tops. The perfect place, in fact, for whiling away the sunny, summer afternoon.

Elmore, close to the sailing club, in the thirties. It was then a popular bathing place from the beach.

Lee sea front, c. 1929. The massed cars have brought in spectators eager to watch the Schneider Cup Trophy Race.

The sea-water pool at the foot of the Clifflands, west of the tower, c. 1932. There seems to be a swimming gala or diving contest in progress. The pool was 240 feet long and 40 feet wide, at least three times the length of today's publics swimming pools.

No resort worth its salt is without a sailing club and this is Lee's smart club house with an uncluttered Portsmouth Road on the right, *c.* 1930.

Lee-on-the-Solent Golf Club House in the sixties.

Four

Business and Shopping

A contemporary photograph of the Marine Parade, Pier Street shops and flats complex. These date from the mid-thirties and are typical of the architecture of the period. Surprisingly, many of the horizontal glazing bars in the apartments still remain in situ.

An attractive photograph of the previous complex in 1950. The heavy snow complements the whiteness of the buildings.

High Street, *c.* 1930. Lee between the wars had many unmade roads. On one occasion some shopkeepers joined together and hired a steam roller to have gravel rolled along the road! At the top left of the photograph is what appears to be Smeed and Smeeds off licence. At top right are the Gas Company offices and Bulson's Retreat, a well-established general and grocery store for many years.

The shop front of Hern and Barlow. This high class grocery store opened in 1951 at No.s 148 to 150 High Street. We see Mr and Mrs J. Hern with furry friend at the entrance. The Herns lived in the flat over the shop.

The Strawberry Workshop is the building once occupied by Hern and Barlow's high class grocers.

Some of the staff of Hern and Barlow. Mr Barlow is third from the right. Every Christmas a moving train set was on show in the shop window, a great attraction for Dads! In the fifties, there were seven grocers' shops in Lee all doing good business when the High Street was a thriving commercial community.

Some of the closely stocked shelves inside Hern and Barlow's high class grocers. The shop sold specialist delicatessen food, which included tinned frogs' legs, chocolate coated ants, fried grasshoppers and silk worms. In 1956, one hundred and forty different cheeses were in stock and orders were shipped world wide. King Haakon of Norway enjoyed Hern and Barlows' Stilton cheese. The shop closed in 1965, facing competition in the advent of the supermarkets.

A perspective of High Street shop fronts. In the forties and fifties the street had a range of specialist shops covering all aspects of the retail trade.

The Spinnaker Café is among the best of Lee's attractive thirties' buildings.

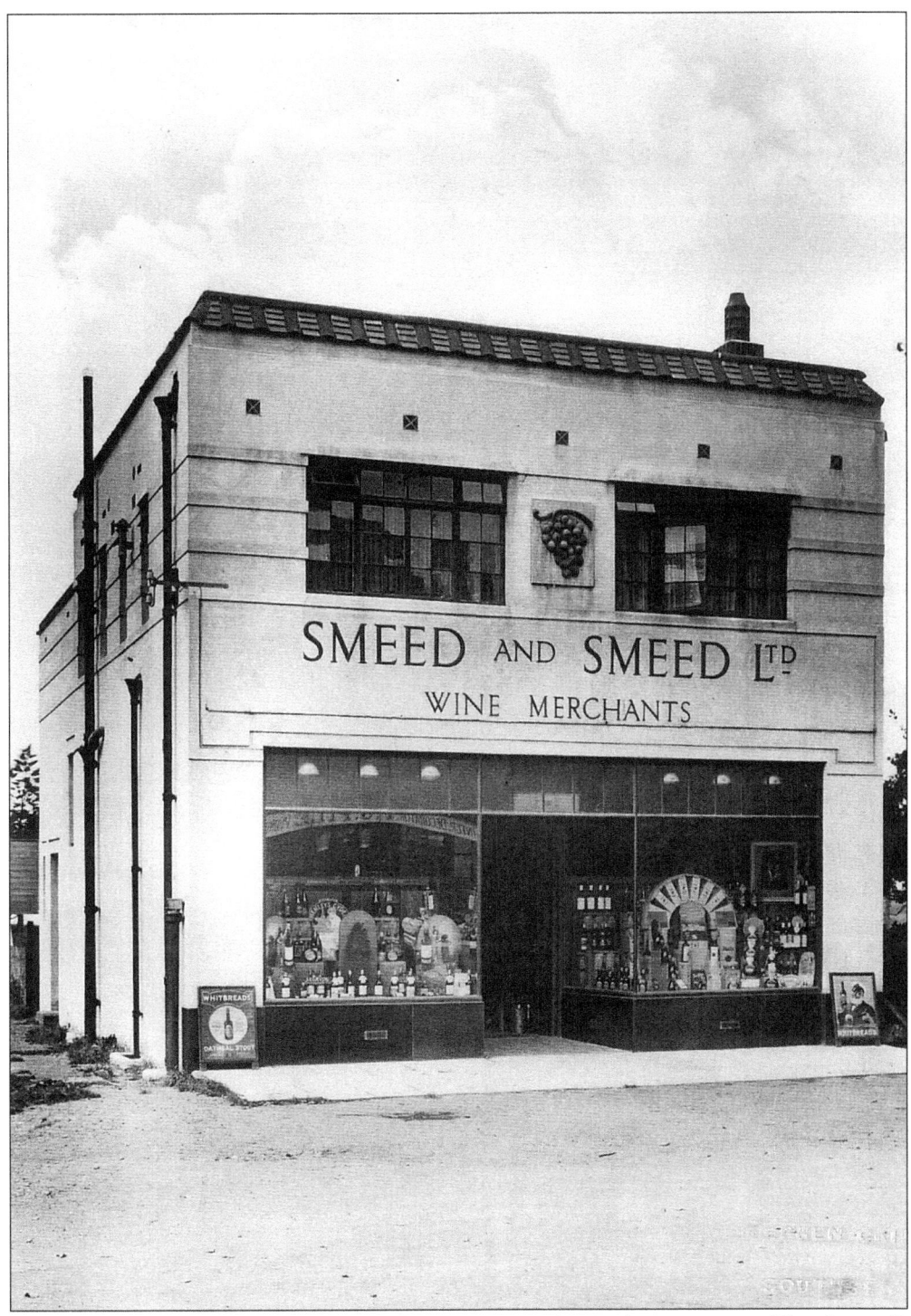

Smeed and Smeed's elegant thirties style premises in the High Street, now Threshers off-licence. Note the decorative bunch of grapes over the entrance. These premises were conveyed to Brickwoods in 1929 for the sum of £500.

⚜ THE "VICTORIA" HOTEL ⚜

(Fully Licensed),

Is now open, and affords comfortable accommodation for Visitors.

A BOWLING GREEN and LAWN TENNIS GROUND are attached.

The Grand Naval Reviews of 1887 and 1889 and the French Fleet during its stay in Osborne Bay in August, 1891, were admirably seen from the Cliffs and Pier at Lee-on-the Solent.

THE "VICTORIA" HOTEL.

An advertisement for the Victoria Hotel, (now the Bun Penny), 1894.

Solent View Guest House

18, MARINE PARADE WEST
LEE-ON-SOLENT, HANTS.

Facing Sea - Magnificent views of the Isle of Wight
7 miles from Southsea
Near Southampton, New Forest and Bournemouth
Golfing, Fishing, Boating and Bathing all available
Sunny Rooms with Balcony - - - Bath (H. & C.)

Inclusive Terms from 2½ guineas

An advertisement for guest house accommodation taken from a guide book of the fifties.

Five

The Lee Tower Saga

The Tower, photographed at a somewhat romantic angle, symbolising the high hopes the developers had for this bold thirties' enterprise.

Foundation work began in 1934 to prepare the Clifflands for the construction of the Tower complex. The workmen dug with spades, no mechanical diggers were used.

The main building contractor was Mr A. Prestidge of Birmingham House, Lee-on-the-Solent. His workforce here is well-advanced on the structural foundations.

The complex is halfway towards completion and the characteristic thirties' architectual style is taking shape.

TOWER CINEMA :

THE OPENIN

THURSDAY, DECEN

1.   National Anthem

2.   **OPENING CEREMONY**

by

Admiral Sir ARTHUR WAISTELL

Assisted by His Worship THE MAYOR

3.   A Short Story About

The Lee Tower

4.   Universal News

5.   Comic Color Cartoon

The opening programme for the Lee Tower and Winter Gardens' complex.

PROGRAMME

26th, 1935, at 6 p.m.

SONNIE HALE

in

6. "MARRY THE GIRL"

With

WINIFRED SHOTTER

The sad story of a bright young bachelor's final fling—
and the hilarious complications it brought him !

The funniest breach of promise case anyone ever
imagined.

DAVE APOLLON

and his Romantic Serenaders

in

7. "IN TOWN TO-NIGHT"

With

Stanley Holloway, Jack Barty, Nora Williams,
Etc.

You must see this Radio Musical Comedy
with its host of Celebrated Stars of the
Air, Screen and Stage.

It's 100% Variety !   Mirth and Melody
marvellously mingled !

FOREWORD

THE MANAGEMENT ask you to accept this Souvenir Programme of the opening of the Lee Tower Cinema, as a token of the very warm welcome they are glad to offer you.

It will be recognised that a Cinema providing first-class entertainment, Comfort and Decoration second to none, perfect reproduction by the latest Western Electric Equipment, and a consistent standard of interest and quality, fulfils a need that has been long-felt in the District.

Col. WILLIAMS

Major FLETCHER (Chairman).

GEO. LILLEY.

MODERN SERVICE

A full staff, whose motto will be courtesy and ready assistance in all matters, has been engaged to render attentive service to patrons.

Suggestions from patrons as to any manner in which their comfort and convenience can be studied still further will be welcomed by the Management, and, if found practicable, put into operation.

It was forty years after the Victorian concept of Lee that the Tower complex was opened. With benefit of hindsight we can feel that the developers had missed the boat. The passenger railway service was discontinued in 1931, many roads were still unmade and war was looming.

CONSTRUCTION

THE Cinema forms part of one of the most magnificent and imposing edifices in the South of England, which in the near future will be known throughout the Country.

Its origin is entirely due to the enterprise and courage displayed by the Chairman of Solent Properties, Ltd., Colonel J. Williams, C.B.E., V.D., who seeing the astounding position of Lee-on-Solent as a modern Seaside resort, determined to build such a structure that any king would be pleased to claim as theirs.

The Architecture and Designing was entrusted to one of the most eminent firms of architects in the country, namely, Messrs. Yates, Cook & Darbyshire, of 43, Great Marlborough Street, London, who are to be congratulated upon the majestic and stately lines of the Building.

Mr. A. PRESTIDGE
(General Contractor).

The whole structure comprising of the Cinema, Dance Hall, Restaurant, Lounge, and Saloon Bars, with a perfect Roof Terrace, and rising above it all, the Lee Tower itself, fitted with a luxury passenger lift to convey patrons to the 120 ft. high platform, which gives an unrivalled sea view of the Solent and Channel. It has been erected by one of our best-known Builders and Townsmen, Mr. A. Prestidge, of Lee-on-Solent, and it need hardly be added, that it will remain as a Monument of craftsmanship and energy to him for all time.

Brave words indeed! The Tower complex was probably before its time and did not survive to herald the beginning of the leisure industry. The thirties architecture would be in tune with today's feeling for heritage.

Winifred Shotter, one of the leading stars of stage and screen in the thirties. She appeared in the Lee Tower's opening concert in 26 December 1935.

Lee Tower Cinema

FOR YOUR INFORMATION

General Manager :
GEO. LILLEY.

Telephone :
79386

The Tower is easily accessible. All Buses stop at the covered entrance to the Vestibule.

CONTINUOUS PERFORMANCE DAILY 1.3 p.m. to 10.45 p.m.

ADMISSION PRICES

(including Tax)

SEATS	PRICES
DRESS CIRCLE	1/10
BACK CIRCLE	1/6
FRONT STALLS	6d.
MIDDLE STALLS	9d.
BACK STALLS	1/-

Telephone : 79386.

Car Park : The Car Park—Free to patrons, is at the rear of the Cinema.

Refreshments : Chocolates, Ices, Cigarettes, etc., on sale in the Cinema.

Monthly Programme : A bright informative periodical forwarded regularly and posted free. Please leave your name and address at the Box Office.

Elegance and comfort were the key features of this little cinema. The 'Art Deco' style of the thirties is very evident. Although intimate in its feel, it could seat 950 people.

The Winter Garden was in fact a very fine ballroom with one of the few sprung floors in the area. It was used for a variety of civic and private functions for many years.

THE TOWER, LEE-ON-SOLENT

The Tower was 120 feet high with an observation platform reached by a lift. Slender and white, it reminded the architectural historian, Nikolaus Pevsner, of an elongated cigarette lighter. He also thought it 'jazzy' with 'a rather nice, elegant vulgarity'.

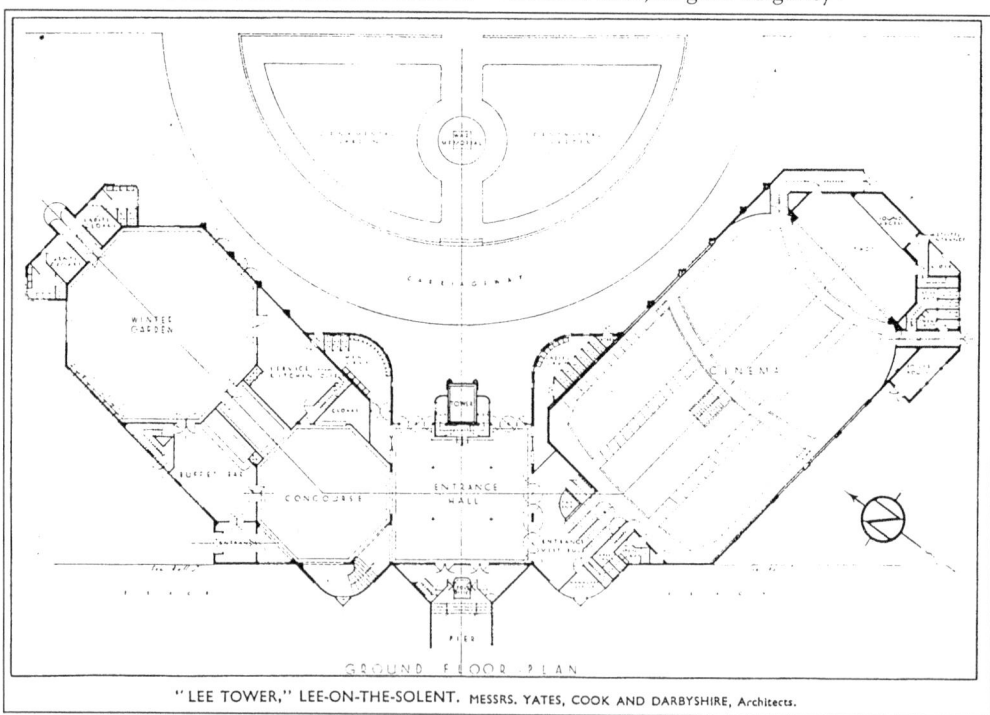

"LEE TOWER," LEE-ON-THE-SOLENT. MESSRS. YATES, COOK AND DARBYSHIRE, Architects.

The layout plans of the Tower development.

The Tower, resplendent in its decorations for Queen Elizabeth II's coronation, 1953. Note that the clock is missing.

Lee Tower, Lee-on-Solent, still sporting remnants of its World War II camouflage.

A post-1945 view of Lee Tower. Youthful swimmers are enjoying their use of the beach after the restrictions of the war years. During D-Day preparations, the Tower complex was the HQ for CO-TUG, the Anglo-American unit responsible for organising transport of Mulberry Harbour components to the Normandy coast.

The Tower, looking east, showing tiered walkway and promenade. The buildings have again assumed their original glistening white elevations after wartime camouflage.

The Tower will never again look as good as it does here. By 1960, its financial losses were a matter of concern for the Borough Council.

The Tower in the fifties. Already, visual street clutter is undermining its elegance.

Looking east towards the Tower. This is the sixties and the Tower is doomed.

Demolition of the Tower. In spite of heroic efforts on the part of the Borough Council and outside consultants, the Tower complex continued to lose money over a period of thirty years. Various gimmicks were employed to promote use of the Tower. These included the Hover Bar; (the world's first hovercraft bar), the Winkle Barge; (which served fresh seafood daily), the Skyline Music Lounge over looking the Solent, the China Garden restaurant, the Bodega Espagnol (a Spanish gypsy bar), together with the usual seaside facilities of snack bars, gift shops, children's amusements and more latterly, ten pin bowling. It was further suggested to turn the Tower into a marina. Two other proposals were for a new central library or a medical centre. Toppling of Lee Tower was finally effected in the Spring of 1971, so ending any dreams of Lee becoming the Monte Carlo of the South.

Six

Wings Over Lee

The origins of the Royal Naval Air Station at Lee can be traced to June 1927, when the seaplane training school at Calshot was looking for more space. H. M. Naval Seaplane Training School was officially opened on 30 July 1917 with initially just two officers and thirty men.

Four seaplanes at the ready. The buildings on the left of the picture are still there today.

Seaplanes wheeled on trolleys from their hangars. Here they were transferred by crane from the cliff edge onto a similar trolley on the beach which ran on rails into the sea.

Looking inside the hangar by the main slip way, with seaplanes receiving attention.

Inside one of the hangars. Servicemen are attending to a Bristol Bailey seaplane.

Getting reading for take-off from the Clifflands.

Supermarine Walruses on the slipway. These planes were affectionately known as 'Shagbats' or 'Steam Pigeons'.

Seaplanes along the shoreline, c. 1918. This picture gives a good impression of the old Clifflands.

Children watch the actions of the men hauling the seaplane.

Local girls rest on their handlebars to watch the seaplanes being hauled up the cliff by means of the special crane, just visible in this picture, *c.* 1918.

Another view of the lifting gear on the Clifflands.

Five men haul in a damaged seaplane.

Curious spectators watch a damaged plane being brought ashore, c. 1918. In 1919 the base was renamed the R.A.F. Seaplane School, Lee-on-the-Solent.

On 24 May 1939, RAF Lee-on-the-Solent was returned to Admiralty control and was commissioned as *HMS Daedalus*. King George VI reviews the WRNS in 1940.

On the same visit, King George VI meets officers and crews of the Swordfish planes.

The WRNS' queue at HMS *Daedalus*.

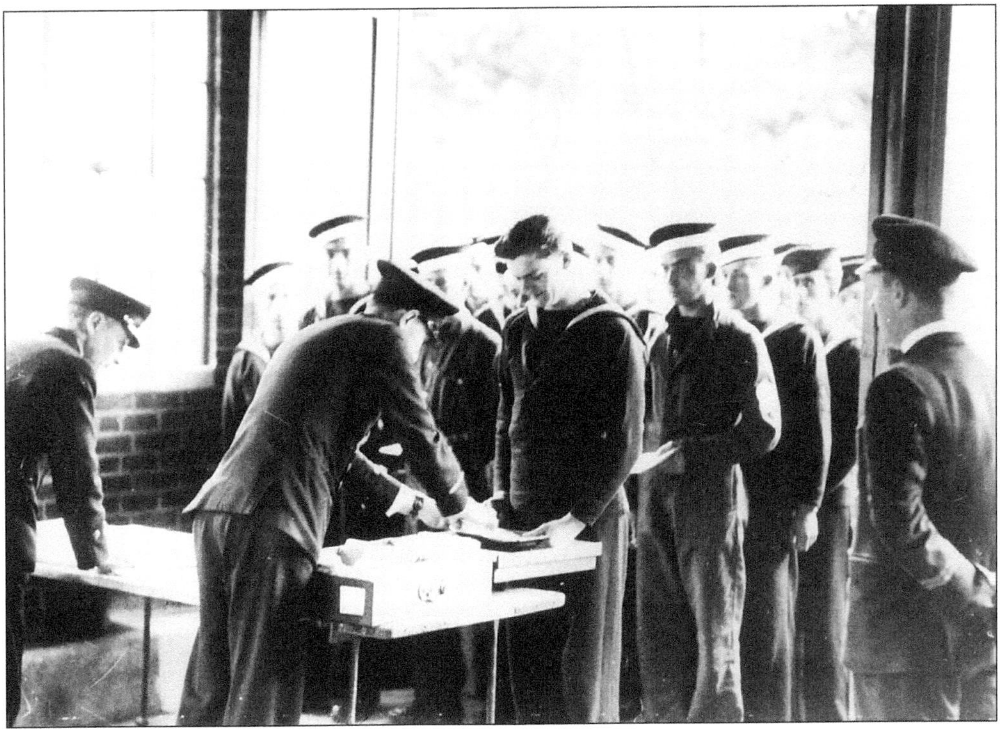

Similarly, the mens' pay queue at HMS *Daedalus*.

Feeding the fliers in the cookhouse at *HMS Daedalus*.

'Stand Easy' for a group of trainee officers.

Service women at *HMS Daedalus* on vital repair work. Note the Singer sewing machine.

Women technicians at work in a hangar at *HMS Daedalus*.

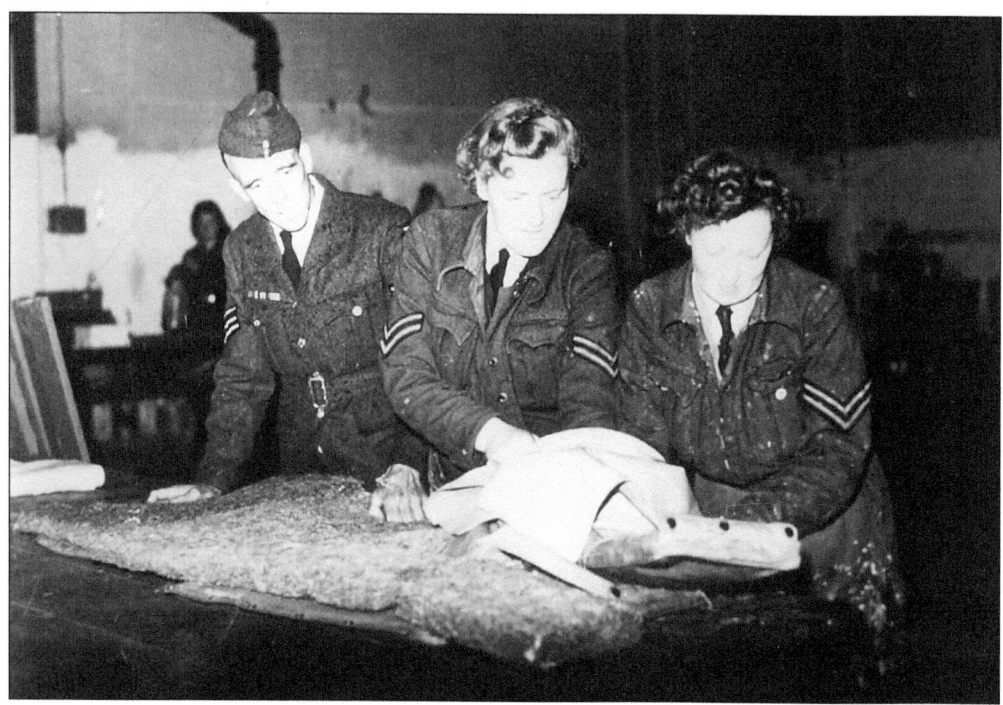

Learning to pack a parachute under the watchful eye of the RAF sergeant.

Serious bomb damage at HMS *Daedalus*, 16 August 1940. Three hangars and forty-two aircraft were destroyed, but there were no casualties. Sadly, on the night of 23 November 1940, eight WRNS were killed when their Lee billet was bombed. The girls are buried in the R.N. Haslar cemetery, Gosport.

Queen Elizabeth II presents the Queen's Colour to *HMS Daedalus* on 30 July 1956. Three years later *HMS Daedalus* is re-named *HMS Ariel*, to more clearly reflect its electrical, radar and ground radio training emphasis.

An impressive line-up of helicopters on the Lee Airfield in celebration of the Queen's silver jubilee in 1977.

The joint Service Hovercraft Unit was formed in 1962 with the aim of testing hovercraft in an operational military environment. Twenty years later, partly due to defence cut-backs the unit was closed. This picture dates from June 1994 when residents and holidaymakers watch the giant SRN 4 'Swift' come up the slipway to be saved for the future planned Hovercraft Museum.

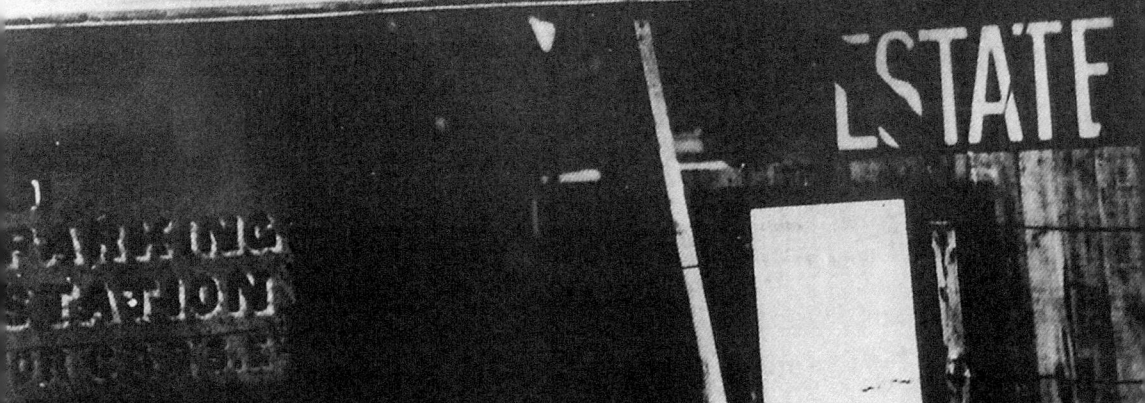

THIS IS LEE ON THE SOLENT "Where the RAINBOW EN

WHAT TO SEE IN OUR VILLAGE

TRAGIC EXAMPLES OF EXTRAVAGANT WASTE OF PUBLIC MONEY.

MAGNIFICENT MANSIONS FOR OFFICERS ONLY *Known as*

WESTCLIFF With Fruit & Flower Gardens WYKEHAM HALL *& Grounds* MANOR WAY GRANGE *with Gardeners Lodge*

18 OTHER HOUSES. ——— NOT FOR THE PEOPLE

All of these are fitted with Electric Light from large private Plant

own Playing Fields, Tennis Courts, Squash Racquet Courts Billiards & Games Room Gymnasium Shoemakers Sho
Greenhouses Etc Etc

The Finest Seaside Club on the Sunny South Coast. *Entry Free with large salaries for Office*

UPKEEP ENORMOUS AT TAXPAYERS EXPENSE

Although unsuitable for Seaplanes. Reconstructed & Lengthened Slipway is Costly & still unsatisfa
We live here & we know

Plus ça change. This hoarding dates from the thirties as local people protested against the expansion of the airfield. 'The end of the rainbow' came for *HMS Daedalus* on 31 March 1996.

Seven

Lee Past and Present

Lee was amalgamated into the Borough of Gosport in 1930. This is the boundary ceremony that took place on 1 April of that year. The mayor of Gosport was Councillor C.E. Davis.

The original St Faith's church, the little Victorian 'tin hut', which sold for £20.

St Faith's Church, Victoria Square, built in 1933. It was designed by the architects Seeley and Paget and won praise from the architectural historian, Nikolaus Pevsner: 'It is demure outside, rose-red brick walls, white framed windows, little bell cote over end gable, as if designed for a "garden city." ' The church was listed at Grade II by the Department of National Heritage in February 1997.

The foundation laying ceremony for St Faith's on 6 May 1932. Bishop Neville Lovett conducts the ceremony in the presence of the incumbent Revd Douglas Hunter.

The opening ceremony for the new Lee public library in November 1937. The library will celebrate its sixtieth anniversary in November 1997.

The Pier Hotel. Here a car and a cyclist proceed westwards along Marine Parade. The Union Jack flies in the hotel forecourt.

A frontal view of the Pier Hotel, showing the Dutch-gabled elevations and what appears to be the wide open spaces in front. The railway station was just across the road, perfect for holidaymakers.

The Pier Street shops and apartment blocks. Here we are looking towards Manor Way in the distance, with its fine mature elm trees and countrified aspect. A horse bus makes its way towards the beach.

Pier Street looking south towards the sea. The shopkeepers have gathered outside their premises to welcome the photographers whose publicity shots would be good for their businesses. This charming piece of Victorian development is part of the Pier Street conservation area.

The Russell and Petrie Roads in the thirties. They are hardly recognisable today with so much infill development. Residential building went on steadily during this period, but the roads and pavements were left unmade, in some cases, until after the Second World War.

IN MANOR WAY.

(The Old Main Road to the Sea). Building line set back 25 feet.

LOT 3

A VERY VALUABLE CORNER PLOT

OF

FREEHOLD BUILDING LAND

With the exceptionally long frontage of 95ft. and depth of 138ft., suitable for the erection of a detached villa residence. (Building value £500).

ON THIS LOT ARE SOME FINE OLD ELM TREES.

LOT 4

A LARGE AND VALUABLE PLOT

OF

Freehold Building Land,

With the important frontage of 80ft. and unusual depth of 292ft. (Building value £500).

Building line set back 40 feet.

An extract from a sale catalogue, 1894. Manor Way is the oldest road in Lee, it is the route of the medieval track to the villages of Stubbington and Titchfield.

Edinburgh House, *c. 1900*. This comprised of a group of houses in Manor Way built in 1898. It was a school for boys and was finally closed down in 1938.

These houses in Manor Way formed the original Edinburgh House and school.

Dean house in Manor Way, one of Lee's substantial Victorian-cum-Edwardian residences. Manor Way boasts many of these fine houses, a number of which have now been converted into apartments. Dean House was occupied by Admiral Nugent during the Second World War. There was also a Dean Cottage situated in its extensive grounds.

LEE BRITTEN FARM.

A Mediæval Farm House of the time of Elizabeth (1558-1603) in an excellent state of preservation.

Farm House Teas, etc., served in Old-World surroundings.

Le Breton farm in the early years of this century. It is of medieval origin and in recent history served as a tea room.

Le Breton farm today, a private residence. In the early years of this century, the old Norman name Le Breton was anglicized to Lee Britten. It is known today as Le Breton.

Some of the substantial Victorian villas along the Marine Parade, *c.* 1905. Marine Parade was specifically designed to give prime views across the Solent. It is a mile long and approximately 150 feet wide.

Marine Parade looking west in the eighties. The roads are made up, but the street clutter of signs and public notices destroy the elegance of the 1905 Marine Parade.

The ceremony for the unveiling of the First World War memorial, *c.* 1920.

The war memorial as it is today. Its present position was the former courtyard in front of Lee Tower.

Lee County Primary school. This opened on 28 September 1908, replacing an earlier temporary building on this site where ninety-seven children had been in the care of one teacher. On 9 July 1912 pupils enjoyed a half-day's holiday to watch the Naval Review at Spithead. There were many opportunities at Lee for watching spectacles, such as the end of the 'Cape to Cairo flight' at Lee aerodrome on 28 June 1926. Children were often absent from school, not only through sickness, but through the need to help with the harvest.

Children of Lee-on-the-Solent Council school, 1925.

Children of the Lee Primary school, 1949. The head teacher was still Mr Nixon in 1947 but was succeeded by Mr A. Ludlow Fisher until 1958 when Mr B. Bird took over the headship.

Front elevations of the wardroom block at HMS *Daedalus*. It is said to have been designed by Sir Edwin Lutyens.

Westcliffe House and the wardroom are the most impressive buildings on the former Ministry of Defence airfield. They were opened to the public for the first time during the Heritage Days' Scheme of 1992.

The Belle Vue Hotel, a more streamlined building than it was in the forties when the advertisement below appeared in the holiday guide.

A Few Reasons why you should stay
at the

BELLE VUE HOTEL
LEE-ON-THE-SOLENT

ON THE SEA FRONT.

1. Unrivalled Cuisine.
2. Comfortable beds, all rooms exceptionally well furnished.
3. Hot and cold water, gas and electric fires in all bedrooms. Central heating.
4. The only Hotel commanding an uninterrupted view of the Isle of Wight and shipping entering the Solent.
5. Sun parlour.
6. Private lock-up garages.
7. Infra-red Ray Treatment available.
8. Five minutes from 18-hole golf course.

MODERATE TERMS.

Proprietors : Mr. & Mrs. CHARLES G. WEBB.

The Inn By The Sea was opened on 19 July 1926, making a handsome addition to Lee's hostelries.

Cornerways, at the junction of Portsmouth Road and Queens Road. This attractive house was built in 1934 and was originally tea rooms, owned and managed by the Misses Triggs. It was a popular venue for service people during the Second World War.

An aerial photograph of Lee in 1935. Portsmouth Road runs across the middle of the picture, Queens Road is in the centre leading to the beach. The Inn By The Sea, Cornerways and the Downing's garage are at the junction of Portsmouth Road, Queens Road and Elmore Road. In the top left of the picture is Common Barn farm. In the bottom foreground is the chopped off railway line. In 1935, the last goods train ran, which saw the end of the railway link to Lee-on-the-Solent.

Shangri-La, Milvil Road is one of Lee's many thirties buildings. This one has the characteristic flat roof with a viewing or observation balcony.

A side view of Shangri-La. The building, made of concrete, with its original flat roof was completed in 1934. Its romantic name probably derives from the James Hilton novel *Lost Horizon* published in 1933. Shangri-La was the Utopian ideal for longevity and the house today now offers residential care for the elderly.

Court Barn Conservative Club now occupies this sixteenth century farm house, an important medieval building. It was held by many significant local families who oversaw the common tenants and small holders of the manor of Le Breton.

The house is listed at Grade II by the Department of National Heritage. It lost its great timbered Court Barn which has now been re-erected at Singleton Weald and Downland Museum and preserved for prosperity.

A nostalgic last look at Elmore beach. In the background can be seen the soon-to-be defunct Elmore Halt while local children sit on the beach under the watchful eye of one of their mothers.

Acknowledgements

Grateful thanks are due to those kind people who allowed us access to their private collections of photographs and to their memories of the Lee-on-the-Solent of the past. We would also like to thank the staffs of Gosport Museum, Gosport Town Hall and Gosport and Lee-on-the-Solent libraries for the use of their collections and facilities accorded to us.

Special thanks to Mr Bill Adams, Mr Bernard Collins, Mr Phillip Eley, Mrs Joan Hadley, Mrs Doris Hern, Mr Nick Redman - Archivist of Whitbreads Plc, Mr Brian Russell, Mr John Sadden, Laurence and Mrs Sandra Smith, Lt. Cdr. M. Thomas - RN of HMS *Collingwood*, Mrs Pen Viret and Mr and Mrs P. Whiffing.

Lesley A. Burton and Beryl F. Peacey
July 1997

Bibliography

The Max Lock Report (1947) Hampshire County Council

The story of Gosport by Lesley Burton and Brian Musselwhite. Ensign Publications (1988)
The story of Lee-on-the-Solent by Ron Brown, Milestone Publications (1982)

Gosport Borough Council minutes 1929 -1970

Naval Aviation at Lee-on-the-Solent by Lt. Cdr. M. Thomas, RN. Gosport Printing Press (1995)

Buildings of Hampshire and the Isle of Wight by N. Pevsnor. Penguin (1967)